Major Tom's

Tarot of Marseilles

Tom Schick

Schiffer Publishing Ltd

4880 Lower Valley Road · Atglen, Pennsylvania · 19310

Published by Schiffer Publishing Ltd.
4880 Lower Valley Road
Atglen, PA 19310
Phone: (610) 593-1777; Fax: (610) 593-2002
E-mail: Info@schifferbooks.com
For the largest selection of fine reference books on this and related subjects, please visit our web site atWe are always looking for people to write books on new and related subjects. If you have an idea for a book please contact us at the above address.
This book may be purchased from the publisher.
Include $3.95 for shipping.
Please try your bookstore first.
You may write for a free catalog.
In Europe, Schiffer books are distributed by
Bushwood Books
6 Marksbury Ave.
Kew Gardens
Surrey TW9 4JF England
Phone: 44 (0) 20 8392-8585; Fax: 44 (0) 20 8392-9876
E-mail: info@bushwoodbooks.co.uk
Website: www.bushwoodbooks.co.uk
Free postage in the U.K., Europe; air mail at cost.

Library of Congress Control Number: 2007929646

Designed by "Sue"
Type set in Florens LP/Humanst521 BT
ISBN: 978-0-7643-2760-5
Printed in China

Dedications and Acknowledgements

I dedicate this tarot deck to my departed father Major Thomas Edward Schick.

I wish to express my deep gratitude to my beloved partner, Jane Christy, for her unstinting help and support throughout the creation of this deck. I could not have done it without her.

My thanks to Jean-Michel David and the Association for Tarot Studies to the supreme honour they bestowed on me by publishing a limited edition of 50 copies of a very rough version of Major Tom's Tarot of Marseilles to mark the occasion of the 2005 Melbourne International Tarot Conference.

And last, but certainly not least, my thanks to my friends, the members of that wonderful international tarot community that is the Aeclectic Tarot Forums, for their valuable insights while

I was creating this deck and the honour they did me by voting the limited addition published by the Association for Tarot Studies number 8 in the Top Ten Decks Published in 2005.

Introduction

For centuries when someone spoke about tarot, they were speaking about the *Tarot of Marseilles*. Even though there were (and are) other decks of cards with tarot in the title, by the 1700s, the pattern we now call the *Tarot of Marseilles* had become recognised as the standard tarot.

By the late nineteenth century, this began to change, with much being written about tarot and new decks being produced. In 1909, Arthur Edward Waite and Pamela Coleman Smith changed everything with the publication of the *Rider Waite Smith Tarot*, a tarot deck with scenic illustrations on the pip cards. *Rider Waite Smith Tarot* remains the best-selling tarot deck in English-speaking countries, despite the hundreds now published every year. Following these innovations, the *Tarot of Marseilles* and related patterns have fallen into comparative obscurity.

Major Tom's Tarot of Marseilles is my attempt to reintroduce the English-speaking world to this wonderfully simple and surprisingly deep tarot pattern. The only changes from the traditional iconography are:

1. The clothing the characters wear, and
2. The gradient backgrounds.

Instead of the traditional medieval clothing, I've dressed the characters in clothing we would see on people in the twenty-first century. As we no longer see monarchs wearing their crowns, the only character to wear a crown in *Major Tom's Tarot of Marseilles* is the Empress. When we see world leaders on television visiting hot countries, they wear baseball caps, so baseball caps have replaced crowns on all the cards.

Traditionally, the *Tarot of Marseilles* was printed with carved blocks of wood, and this limited how the characters could be drawn. I've tried to retain that same feel. The cards in *Major Tom's Tarot of Marseilles* were drawn in 4H pencil on A4 size paper. The drawings were then inked with ball point pen before being scanned into a computer. The colours and gradient backgrounds were added using Paint Shop Pro 8. I feel this method helped maintain the "woodblock" feel, yet acknowledge that twenty-first century printing methods allow greater flexibility.

It's my hope that these simple alterations to the ancient iconography will help twenty-first century people see the relevance of the *Tarot of Marseilles* to their everyday lives. It is my firm belief that it is as fresh and relevant now as it was in that lost time when it was first created.

It would be entirely unfair to produce a tarot deck hoping to appeal to people who know nothing about tarot, as well as those who do, without also providing some instruction in their use. There is a school of thought that would suggest that all one needs is the cards themselves.

Jean-Michel David has written, "The instrument is its own teacher."

In many ways, there is much to be said for just looking at the cards, and yet, there are those who find that instruction may be necessary.

Paul Foster Case, in his book, *The Tarot,* quotes Eliphas Levi as writing, "As an erudite Kabalistic book, all combinations of which reveal the harmonies pre-existing between signs, letters and numbers, the practical value of the Tarot is truly and above all marvellous. A prisoner devoid of books had he only a Tarot of which he knew how to make use, could in a few years acquire a universal science, and converse with an unequalled doctrine and inexhaustible eloquence."

Reading Tarot

There is a spectrum or continuum of methods for reading tarot. At one end is the idea that each card has an "assigned set" of meanings that have been agreed over the centuries. At the other end of the spectrum is the idea that one can look at a card in a given context and "intuit" the meaning from what attracts one's attention. Most tarot readers will operate from somewhere in between these two extremes.

I will attempt to give the reader the minimum needed, so that with *Major Tom's Tarot of Marseilles*, one will know how to make use of the cards.

The Steps

The first step anyone should take in learning about tarot is to attempt to find a study partner. This can be anyone who shares your interest, and need not be an expert, only someone with whom to share a fascinating journey of discovery. Although a class led by a professional can be a very worthwhile experience, it isn't necessary to learning to read tarot. Indeed, in this internet age, your study partner needn't be in the same room and could be thousands of miles away. It is only necessary that you are able to communicate in some fashion about your experiences with the cards. There really is no reason to try to learn alone.

The next step is to acquire a notebook for your tarot studies. Think of it as your tarot journal and you can organise it in any way that you see fit. The day you start your tarot study, pick out a single card from your deck and make note of it in your journal. Record your thoughts and impressions about the card. Do this every day. Try to pick out one card at the same time every day. You can also return to the previous day's card and record your reflections on that card. Continue with this practice until you've recorded impressions for all the cards. Many students find this practice so valuable that they continue with it indefinitely.

There are 78 cards in a tarot deck. These are divided into 22 trump cards, 40 pip cards and 16 court cards. We will deal with this each in turn, but first, we'll consider both numbers and colours.

The Colours

All the cards have bright colours, and one can get meaning from those colours. Here are a few keywords for the colours. You can also get your own impression from them.

- **Red - passion, danger, energy, war, sex, love, and desire.**
- **Orange - enthusiasm, fascination, creativity, determination, attraction, success, encouragement, and stimulation.**
- **Yellow - joy, happiness, intellect, honour, loyalty, and warning.**
- **Green - growth, harmony, freshness, fertility and safety.**
- **Blue - wisdom, faith, spirituality, truth and understanding.**
- **Purple - royalty, dignity, luxury, ambition, mystery, and magic.**
- **White - purity, light, goodness, mercy, innocence and virginity.**
- **Black - power, formality, evil, death and mystery.**

The Numbers

The only cards that do not have numbers are *The Fool* and the court cards. All the other cards have numbers printed on them, or in the case of the pips, numbers associated with them, so it's useful to have an idea what numbers mean. Numbers have very distinct personalities which become easily identifiable as you become more familiar working with them. Here are a few keywords to get you started:

- One – unity, willpower, all that is
- Two – duality, the other, cooperation, opposition, diplomacy
- Three – nurturing, growth, development, expression
- Four – discipline, solidity, structure
- Five – freedom, variety, conflict

- Six – responsibility, caring, home, service
- Seven – analysis, wisdom, desire for perfection
- Eight – material success, efficiency, justice
- Nine – understanding, completion
- Ten – the next level, end of cycle

The Trumps

Now we can begin to consider the cards themselves, beginning with the trumps. For each of the trumps, I provide a short description and an idea of what the card represents. As you work with the cards in your daily draw you'll begin to make your own associations. This is by no means intended as an exhaustive list, but only enough information to get you started.

I – The Conjuror

Dressed in the top hat and colourful suit we associate with the circus, sideshow, or fairground. He could be running the shell game or selling the latest gadget. "It slices; it dices, but wait until you see this!" He represents an act of will or making something happen.

II – The Papess

Or female pope, wearing the mitre and cape we associate with religious authority; underneath she wears the red bra trimmed with gold and red skirt we might associate with a pole dancer. She holds the book of knowledge and rests her foot upon the wheel. She represents secret knowledge, the four faces of woman and the use of intuition.

III – The Empress

Wearing a colourful shift-style dress, holding her sceptre, with one arm around her shield, she has the look of many a harassed mother. She is in charge of the emotional welfare of the Empire and represents nurturing, motherhood, growth and development.

IIII – The Emperor

Dressed in a shell suit, with trainers and his baseball cap on backwards, he insouciantly leans against his throne. He controls and directs the running of the Empire. He represents structure, discipline, stability, control and decision making.

V – The Pope

Dressed precisely as we see him on television in the robes and mitre, he is God's representative on Earth. Shown with him are two applauding members of the vast audience that gathers around him everywhere he appears. His function is to serve as a bridge between heaven and earth. He represents spiritual authority and group effort.

VI – The Lover

In this card we're witnessing the scene following the wedding reception as the bride and groom depart. To the left is the groom's mother. In the centre is the groom. To the right is the bride. Flying above is Cupid. The scene shows the groom taking leave of his mother to go to live with his wife. The card represents caring, love and the need to make a choice.

VII – The Chariot

Wearing the fire retardant suit as worn by racing car drivers, the Charioteer pauses a moment before continuing movement. With two horses of different colours, pulling in different directions, this card recalls Plato's allegory of the soul. It represents overcoming difficult challenges and victory.

VIII – Justice

A woman wears the robes and wig of a British High Court Judge, holding aloft a sword in one hand and scales in the other. Her left elbow pushes the scales off balance. From earliest experiences on the playground at school, everyone develops an idea of justice or fairness. This card represents fairness, justice, and receiving what one deserves.

VIIII – The Hermit

Dressed in jeans, long sleeve shirt, and long overcoat, he holds aloft a lantern to light the way. He represents wisdom, understanding, and the fullness of time.

X – The Wheel of Fortune

We've got a monkey in a skirt, a jackass in a shirt, and a sphinx in a baseball cap. We can get the sense of the three monkeys, *hear no evil, see no evil and speak no evil*. Sometime you're up and sometimes you're down. The wheel goes 'round and 'round. Represents luck, both good and bad.

XI – Strength

Wearing a summer sun dress and straw hat, she holds the lion's mouth open with the lightest of touches. You can sense that with a simple gesture the lion would attack at her command. Strength is not so much physical strength as it is to control the "fly or fight" instinct.

XII – The Hanged Man

A rugby shirt and jeans with trainers are worn by the Hanged Man. He appears to be suffering with his tongue hanging out, until the card is turned upside down and he appears to be jeering. This card can represent a sacrifice for self or others, or the need to look at things from a different perspective.

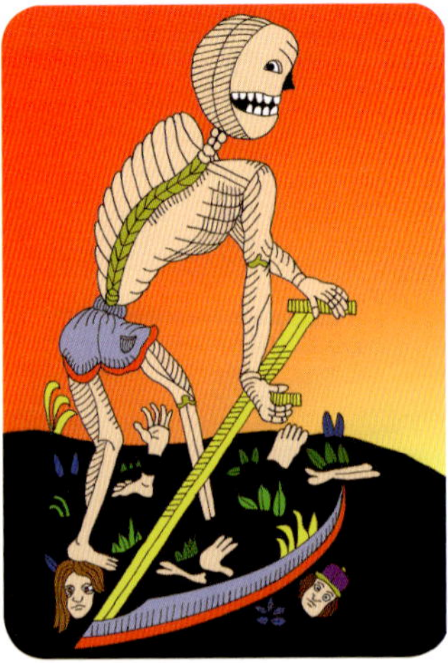

XIII – The trump without a name

A skeleton with a scythe traverses a field filled with body parts and sprouting plants. This trump needs no name because we all know what it is called. This card represents death, transformation, and leaving things behind.

XIIII – Temperance

A buxom, winged angel wearing a prom dress performs a miracle of pouring fluid from one cup to the next. Temperance represents the fusion of two materials or qualities that don't normally go together in order to make something new. We can think in terms of oil and vinegar to make salad dressing or fire and water to forge a sword. Indeed, the sword is tempered by heating in fire and then cooling in water.

XV – The Devil

Wears a visor and antlers while his/her minions wear flat caps. This Devil invites you to join in the fun, hoping you're unwary enough to be hooked on it. Usually represents a trap or restriction which is voluntary.

XVI – The House of God

The baseball cap atop the tower is blown askew. A man in a long sleeve shirt lies at the base of the tower, while another man in a long sleeve shirt and trousers falls to the ground. This card represents the collapse of a long-term view of the self in a blinding flash of insight.

XVII – The Star

A naked woman pours liquid from two vessels onto the water and onto the ground under the stars in the sky. This card represents hope and the grace of God.

XVIII – The Moon

A lobster rises to the surface of the water, while two animals seem to try to catch the sparks falling from the moon on their tongues. Two towers frame the landscape in the background. The Moon represents illusion, the subconscious, and developing psychic awareness.

XVIIII – The Sun

Two children in shorts stand before a wall. The Sun looks on from above. The Sun represents happiness, joy, and innocence. Do be aware that one can get too much sun.

XX – Judgement

A winged angel blows a horn while three figures below seem to rise up from their graves. The scene recalls the Final Judgement from Revelations. This card often represents a "wake up call" or sudden realisation of some importance. One is one's own harshest judge.

XXI – The World

An androgynous figure, with a scarf strategically placed, dances in the centre of a wreath surrounded by a winged man, a bird of prey, a lion and a bull. The entire scene recalls medieval painting of Christ ascending into heaven. The World represents feeling whole and complete.

The Fool

Wears a traditional fool's hat and carries a bag on a long spoon carried over his shoulder. His jeans are torn and he is about to be attacked by an animal as he strides forward looking up into the sky. We can think in terms of the foolish fool or the wise fool. Either he is too inexperienced to recognise the dangers of life, or he is so far advanced that he knows nothing physical can truly harm him.

The Pips

Before we jump in with keywords for the pip cards, it's useful to consider the suit symbols and meanings. In French, the trumps are called *atouts*, the batons are called *bâtons*, cups are called *coupes*, coins are called *deniérs*, and swords are called *épees*. Notice that the names in French are alphabetical. Traditionally, the batons are associated with the peasantry, cups with the clergy, coins with merchants, and swords with the aristocracy.

There are no traditional associations between suit symbols and elements. In fact, one could probably find a tarot deck drawn for every possible combination of associations. It is only through the use of the cards that I have come to associate batons with air, cups with water, coins with earth, and swords with fire. The student is advised not to rush to accept these assignments but to develop one's own associations.

If you have already developed a set of associations, by all means continue to use those.

The following keywords were developed with the class I run in Framlingham, Suffolk, England. We simply constructed a grid with keywords for the suits across the top and keywords for the numbers down the side. By combining the keywords we filled in the grid. I give them here as a list that is by no means exhaustive. The student is advised to develop his or her own meanings through practice. These are simply to get you started.

Aces

Batons

Cups

• Batons – new passion, a surprise opportunity, inspiration

• Cups – the source of unconditional love, the source of all emotion

Aces

Coins

Swords

• Coins – new opportunity for making money, material gain, new job

• Swords – a new idea, a surprise opportunity, a surprise confrontation, inspiration

Twos

Batons

Cups

• Batons – expanding influence, compromise, temporary hold up, conspiracy

• Cups – union, partnership, compatibility, seeing another view, awakening, acceptance

Twos

Coins

Swords

• Coins – choice, balance, investment, work/life balance, trickery

• Swords – indecision, stalemate, of two minds, seeking self-expression, difficult choice

Threes

Batons

Cups

• Batons – seeing the whole picture, possibilities coming together, launching new venture

• Cups – emotional/spiritual support, union, celebration

Threes

Coins

Swords

- Coins – expert at work, just rewards for work
- Swords – revelation, new realisation

Fours

Batons

Cups

• Batons – home, a wedding, celebration, steady job, enjoy the routine

• Cups – boredom, failing to see opportunities, separateness

Fours

Coins

Swords

• Coins – holding on, prudence, regular savings, consolidation

• Swords – stagnation, needing a rest

Fives

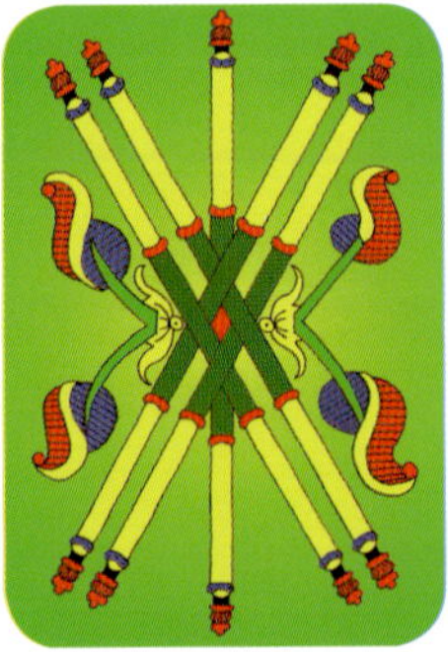

Batons

Cups

- Batons – strife, conflict, blowing off steam, cooperation, working together
- Cups – loss, regret, need to move on, gratitude

Fives

Coins

Swords

• Coins – poverty, beliefs about resources, missed opportunities, the need to ask for help

• Swords – domination, hollow victory, defeat, a bully

Sixes

Batons Cups

• Batons – satisfaction, success, balance, charity work, victory

• Cups – nostalgia, charity, comfort, peace, helping others

Sixes

Coins

Swords

• Coins – charity, generosity, balance of support

• Swords – fleeing to safety, guided forward, finding solutions

Sevens

Batons

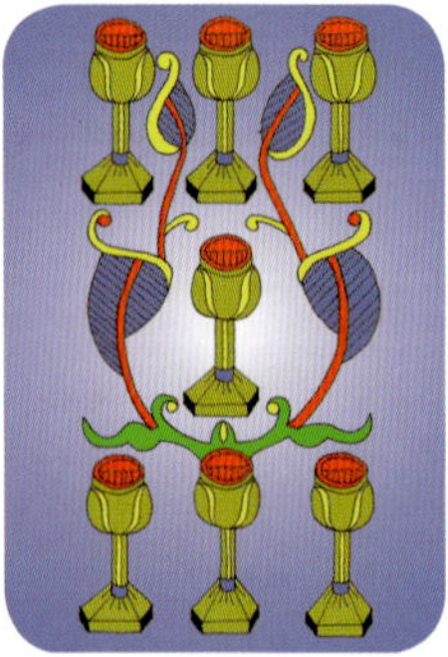

Cups

• Batons – belief in self, affirmation, cooperation, risk taking, conflict/strife

• Cups – soul searching, considering possibilities, seeking the ideal, inner guide

Sevens

Coins

Swords

• Coins – potential, keeping at it, what to do next, changing roles, time to do something new

• Swords – theft, taking a chance, keeping secrets, setting goals, setting ground rules

Eights

Batons

Cups

- Batons – being busy, keep eye on the goal, purpose
- Cups – walking away, turning your back, embarking on a spiritual journey

Eights

Coins

Swords

• Coins – work, steady job, repetition

• Swords – feeling trapped, nearly there

Nines

Batons

Cups

• Batons – duty, a cause worth fighting for, need to care for health, learn from mistakes

• Cups – the wish card, unconditional love, emotional fulfilment

Nines

Coins

Swords

• Coins – material satisfaction, gains, self-reliance, loneliness, isolation

• Swords – sleeplessness, all in one's head, blinded, foresight, revelation, seeing a way clear

Tens

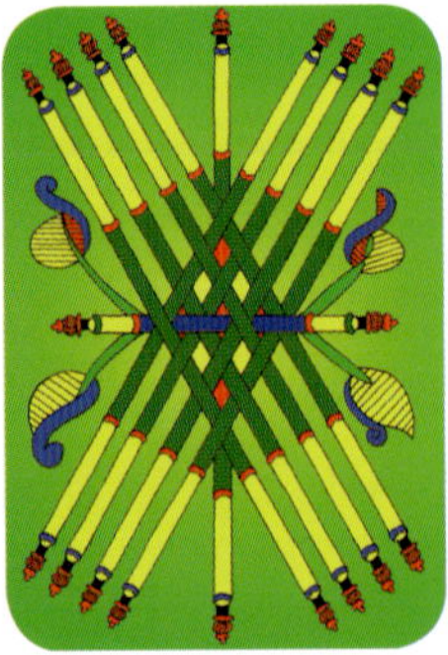

Batons

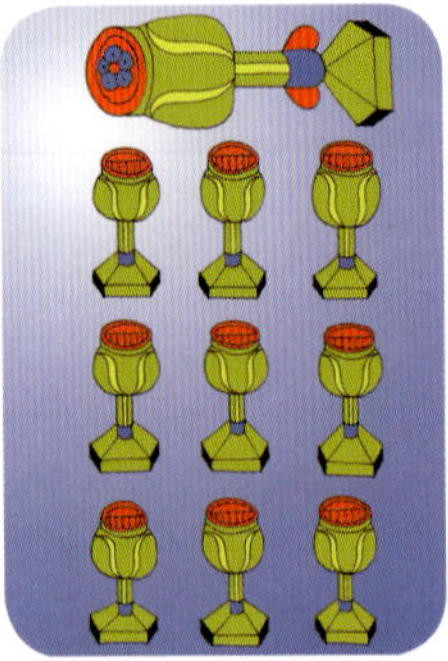

Cups

• Batons – Over-burdened, avid pursuit, clarity of purpose, working smarter

• Cups – happy family, complacency

Tens

Coins

Swords

- Coins – legacy, generations, prosperity
- Swords – betrayal, the worst is over, clarity of thought

Reversals

Some more experienced students will ask about meanings for reversals. It is my thought and way of working that the card itself contains all of its potential meanings whether upright or reversed so I do not split these out.

The Courts

These are the "people" cards, and quite often simply represent people in one's life. Yet, they can also represent qualities or personality traits. You can view these simply in terms of their title and suit. In this system, you assign the following meanings to the titles:

Valets are the *learning* quality,
Cavaliers are the *doing* qualities,
Queens are the *feeling* quality and
Kings are the *controlling* quality.

Combine these meanings with the meanings you have for the suits, and you have meanings for the cards. It really can be that simple.

Nonetheless, I will describe each of the 16 cards, because the clothing they wear helps determine their meaning.

Special Note: The student is reminded that these summaries are just the starting point, and that one will be rewarded for personal reflection on the meanings and usage of the courts. The student may wish to reflect that there are 16 court cards and 16 Myers-Briggs Personality Types or MBTIs. There have been many attempts to create a one-to-one correspondence and each will have flaws, but students might find it enlightening to try for their selves.

Valet of Batons

This card traditionally has no title and shows a man dressed as a tree surgeon. It appears as if he has just trimmed off a branch, which he now holds to offer to you. This Valet offers you the chance to *learn something new*.

Valet of Cups

Dressed in choir robes this Valet carries a cup across uneven ground. He offers you the chance to *learn to love something*.

Valet of Coins

Wears the hat and apron of the baker's assistant or deli counter. He suggests you *learn about investing in yourself.*

Valet of Swords

Wears the uniform of a military cadet. He offers you the chance to *learn about interpersonal interactions.*

Cavalier of Batons

With a ten gallon hat and yoked shirt, this Cavalier is dressed like a cowboy. He leans over as if to hand you his baton. He gives you the opportunity to *do something*.

Cavalier of Cups

His dog collar and his poncho, together with the way he holds his cup, makes you think this Cavalier is on a mission. He suggests *demonstrating commitment to what you love.*

Cavalier of Coins

Wearing clothing for dressage, this is the only Cavalier that does not hold the symbol of his suit. Rather it appears in the air in front of him. He suggests you *work to achieve what you want.*

Cavalier of Swords

Dressed as if for combat or riot control, this Cavalier rides aggressively forward. He suggests you *practice discipline*.

Queen of Batons

Wearing a frilly dress and balancing a baton shaped like a table leg over her shoulder, this Queen invites you to *reflect upon what you intend.*

Queen of Cups

Complete with beret, she's dressed like a member of the flower committee in the local church. She invites you to *empathise with the people and things around you.*

Queen of Coins

Dressed simply in a dress and surrounded by throws, she contemplates the coin she holds up to her eye level. The Queen suggests you *feel comfortable in your own skin.*

Queen of Swords

Her military uniform is formal, and she appears rather casual with her handling of her sword. This queen invites you to *feel the impact of your actions*.

King of Batons

He is dressed casually in short sleeve shirt and trousers. He holds a massive and intricately carved baton. He invites *clarity of thought and vision*.

King of Cups

You'd be forgiven for thinking this King feels the cold, as he's wearing a cap with ear flaps and has a scarf around his neck. He suggests it is a *matter choice how you express your feelings.*

King of Coins

Wearing a jacket, shirt, and tie, this King seems to sink back into his throne. He casually holds his coin and seems to stare off into space. He invites you to *consider your options for the manner in which you live your life.*

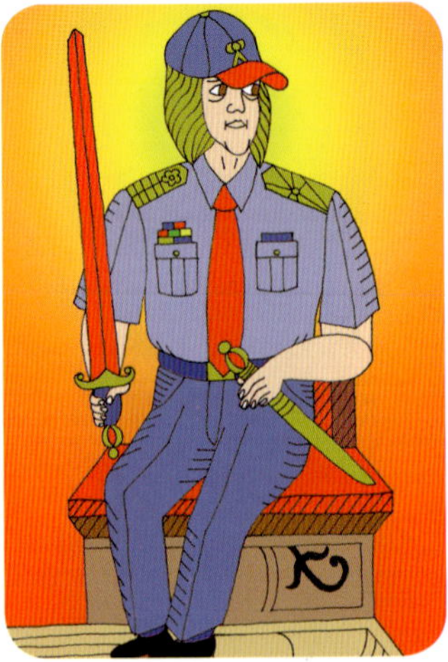

King of Swords

His uniform is short-sleeved, and yet he wears a tie. It is the every-day work uniform. He holds his sword aloft, and yet keeps a dagger handy. He invites you to *be prepared to do what needs to be done to face life's everyday challenges.*

Your First Reading

I'd like to call the tarot an operating manual for a human being. Reading this manual is about learning to be yourself – who you really are.

The truth about the future is that everything you do, everything you say, and everything you think creates your future for you moment to moment.

Tarot helps you shape that future by showing *you* about *you*.

Birth Numbers

For your first reading, you'll need to find your birth number.

Take your birth date and numerologicaly reduce it to a single digit. Your soul card is the corresponding card from the Major Arcana of the tarot.

For example, consider the birth date: 22nd August 1955. Add:

2+2+8+1+9+5+5 = 32 –>3+2
= 5.

Thus, the birth number is: five. This makes the soul card: 5 - The Pope.

Your birth number will be a number in between 1 - 9 inclusive. Just add the digits that make up your birth date. Be sure to include all four digits of the year.

The numbers 1 to 9 correspond to the first 9 trumps I – VIIII.

• A birth number of 1 corresponds to I – The Conjuror

• A birth number of 2 corresponds to II – The Papess

- A birth number of 3 corresponds to III – The Empress
- A birth number of 4 corresponds to IIII – The Emperor
- A birth number of 5 corresponds to V – The Pope
- A birth number of 6 corresponds to VI – The Lover
- A birth number of 7 corresponds to VII – The Chariot
- A birth number of 8 corresponds to VIII – Justice
- A birth number of 9 corresponds to VIIII – The Hermit

Find the card that corresponds to your birth number. I call this card your soul card. What does this card say to *you* about *you*? What do other people say about this card and you? What does this card say to you? Find out and write it in your tarot journal. Talk about it with your tarot study partner.

Meditating and the Cards

Try this very simple, yet surprisingly, deep meditation:

1. Find a quiet space and sit comfortably upright.

2. Hold and study the image of your soul card, until you can see the image in detail in your mind's eye, with your eyes shut.

3. Step into your card. Experience the card with all your senses. What do you see? What do you hear? What do you smell? What can you taste? What can you touch? Interact and speak with the characters you find there. Pay attention to your emotions while you are in this alternative reality. You might ask the characters if they have a message for you.

4. When you are finished, step back out of your card and sit quietly, and slowly return to your sense of your physical surroundings. When you feel completely back in your body, open your eyes.

5. Don't forget to write your experience in your journal.

You can try this meditation with any other card. It is especially effective with the trumps and courts, but will work with the pips too.

Questions

The simplest method of accessing the book that is tarot, is to ask questions. Most readings answer questions whether or not a question was asked. Considering your question is important. You can ask anything at all and get a meaningful answer. Timing can be difficult, but can be built into the question. What do you ask?

Simple, *first person, open* questions work best:

- Who am I?
- Why am I here?
- What is my purpose?
- What do I need to know (today) (this week) (this month) (this season) (this year)?

Questions do not have to be serious:

- What will happen if I put mushrooms in the casserole?
- Will my team win the trophy if I go to the game?

I think the most important questions are goal oriented. What can one do to achieve a goal? Certainly we know tarot can answer questions about the future, but isn't the best use of tarot to *shape* the future?

Some people will want to consult tarot without having a question, and this is possible, too. Many readers will silently ask, "What does this person need to know?" as they lay the cards.

Do consider why you or your client wants to know the answer to this particular question – the ethics of the situation at hand. Love is the law.

Spreads

Spread is the name for a way to lay out the cards for you to interpret. Not everyone uses a spread. They just think of a question and turn over cards until they are happy with the answer. This can take the whole pack or more. There are a great many different spreads in the world, and the one I use most, and beginners find easy, is the 3-card spread.

For a 3-card spread you just select 3 cards at random from the deck and lay them out in what ever pattern you wish. I lay mine in a horizontal row.

Before you lay the cards, decide what the 3 card positions will mean. A very common 3-card spread is the *past, present, future*. The first card represents the past, the second the present, and the third, the future. Another I use often is *situation, advice, and outcome*. Still another could be *snap, crackle and pop*. Snap representing what was broken; crackle what *is* breaking, and pop, the idea to get through. Think of anything that comes in threes. The point is, you can assign any meaning to the 3-card positions before you lay the cards. Write the meanings in your journal or on a piece of paper before you start.

You might wish to think of your question first, then pick position meanings to help answer that question.

I feel strongly that beginners should stick with 3-card spreads, and there are so many sources for them, that I am not going to provide any other spreads here. Use 3-card spreads until you feel entirely comfortable using them. If you already are comfortable with 3-card spreads, then chances are, you'll already have your favourite spreads too.

Putting it all together

You've got your deck and you've got a question. You know you'll use 3 cards. Simply mix the cards by shuffling or mixing them up on the table. You could even simply spread the cards on the table. Pick 3 out, turn them over and read. It really *is* that simple.

What draws your eye? What provokes an emotional response?

Make up a story based on the 3 cards. The cards always tell a story.

Each card will have meanings. The position drawn has meaning. The question provides a framework. Put these elements together to tell the story that illustrates the answer.

Words of wisdom

Try to avoid the temptation to keep asking the same question until you get the answer you want. You will get nonsense eventually. The first reading always has the right answer. If you don't like the answer ask what you can do to change it.

Frequently Asked Questions That Have the Same Answer

1. Do I have to shuffle the cards a certain way?
2. How many times do I shuffle the deck?
3. Do I have to keep my cards wrapped in silk, in a wooden box, on a shelf above my head?
4. Do I need to perform a ritual?
5. Someone touched my deck, do I need to cleanse my deck or charge my deck?

The answer to these questions is:
do what feels right to you.

In general, if anyone tells you that you must or have to do anything in particular when using the tarot, you tell them that I say you can do whatever you feel is right!

Frequently Asked Questions with Different Answers

1. Can I read the cards for myself?

Yes, you can read the cards for yourself. Try to remain detached from any particular answer—which is easy to write here, but difficult in practice.

2. Can I buy my own tarot deck?

Yes, you can buy as many tarot decks as you wish.

3. Can I use a tarot deck someone bought for me?

Yes, you can. The person who bought you the gift might be disappointed if you didn't use it.

4. Can I use someone else's tarot deck?

Yes, you can. You should make sure they know you're going to use their tarot deck beforehand. Some people can be very sensitive about other people using their decks.

5. Is there any spread that deals with a particular question?

There are thousands of spreads written, and some of them deal with particular questions. If you have a particular question, why don't you create your own position meanings for a 3-card spread?

6. Is there a connection between Tarot and religion?

There is no connection per se. That said, tarot can and often does lead one to reflect on one's connection to everything, which can be a deeply spiritual experience.

Online Resources

My website is: http://www.majortom.biz

The international tarot community: http://www.tarotforum.net/index.php?referrerid=491

You can certainly find people to talk about tarot here.

To find a meeting local to you, try here: http://tarot.meetup.com

The Association for Tarot Studies: http://association.tarotstudies.org

Final Words

You have a tarot deck. I've given you the knowledge in these pages to use it. In a few years of continued use, you "will acquire a universal science and converse with and unequalled doctrine and inexhaustible eloquence."

The wonderful thing about tarot is that there is always more to learn.

Enjoy your journey with tarot.